The Poetry School, supported by Arts Council England (London), was founded in 1997 and now has over a thousand people enrolling annually on its courses. Beginning with one Saturday workshop run by Jane Duran and Mimi Khalvati, its activities have expanded into the most comprehensive programme of study in the reading and writing of poetry in the country. Its twelve core tutors are fine poets, writers and critics, and students have also been privileged to work with poets of international standing, such as Jorie Graham, Marilyn Hacker, Galway Kinnell, Paul Muldoon, Les Murray, Charles Simic and C. K. Williams. Without the commitment and thirst for poetry of the participants, none of this would have happened. *Entering the Tapestry* reflects a dimension of their talent, and is dedicated to them all.

Graham Fawcett grew up in South-East London and Sussex, studied Classics at Christ's Hospital, read Archaeology & Anthropology and English at Cambridge, and lived in Italy and Catalonia for five years. He teaches reading courses for The Poetry School and translation at Goldsmiths College, lectures in Italy for Art History Abroad, and writes and broadcasts on literature and music for BBC Radio 3. His translations include Fellini's *Cinecittà* (Studio Vista, 1989) and Dante's *La Vita Nuova* (Radio 3, 1990). He edited *Anvil New Poets* (Anvil Press, 1990).

Mimi Khalvati was born in Tehran and grew up on the Isle of Wight. Her Carcanet collections include *In White Ink* (1991), *Mirrorwork* (1995), for which she received an Arts Council of England Writer's Award, and *Entries on Light* (1997). *Selected Poems* was published in 2000 and her most recent collection, *The Chine*, in 2002. She is founder of The Poetry School and co-editor with Pascale Petit of the School's first anthology of new writing, *Tying the Song* (Enitharmon Press, 2000).

Entering the Tapestry

A second anthology from The Poetry School 2001–2003

EDITED BY MIMI KHALVATI & GRAHAM FAWCETT

ENITHARMON PRESS

First published in 2003
by the Enitharmon Press
26B Caversham Road
London NW5 2DU

www.enitharmon.co.uk

Distributed in the UK by
Central Books
99 Wallis Road
London E9 5LN

Distributed in the USA and Canada
by Dufour Editions Inc.
PO Box 7, Chester Springs
PA 19425, USA

ISBN 1 900564 48 3

Enitharmon Press gratefully acknowledges the
financial support of Arts Council England, London

British Library Cataloguing-in-Publication Data.
A catalogue record for this book is available
from the British Library.

Typeset in Bembo by Servis Filmsetting Ltd
and printed in England by
The Cromwell Press Ltd.

CONTENTS

III

INTRODUCTION

Having reached the final stages of editing and the happy job of typing up the Contents page, we were struck by the number of times the word *from*, indicating a sequence, prefaced selected poems – so many times that, in the interests of travelling light, we decided to drop these *froms* from the body of the book while keeping them on the Contents page.

But what does this word *from* imply? That many of our poets, writing sequences and longer poems, are dealing with complexity and difficulty by giving themselves more space; that they are focused not only on the single poem but on developing a body of work; that they have already found urgent themes that demand revisiting; and that behind the poems in *Entering the Tapestry* lies a wealth of work produced by an ever-growing number of talented writers dedicated not only to the writing but to the study and reading of poetry. It is from this context that we have selected poems from thirty poets. And, of course, from the context of The Poetry School that has welcomed and been enriched by our participants.

Initially, we invited submissions from eighty potential contributors. Their response confirmed the sense we had at the outset that we should keep an open mind as to the nature and shape of this book and that the submissions themselves should tell us whether this second anthology should present *poets*, like its predecessor *Tying the Song*, or *poems*. It quickly emerged that there was a large number of people we wanted to include who were demonstrating a sustained quality of work that could lead to a first collection. We had decided that we would not consider work from those who had already had a first collection published by the time we came to make our selection. Since then, two of our contributors, Chris Beckett and Nadine Brummer, have gone on to have collections accepted by publishers and Nadine's *Half Way to Madrid* is a Poetry Book Society Recommendation. We were also aware that some of the writers we were unable to include this time round may well appear in forthcoming anthologies in this biennial series.

So the book which has finally emerged from this process asks for our thirty poets that they allow themselves to be represented by as few as one to five poems each – despite having an achieved body of work behind them – and to be seen as representing the enormous amount of talent and potential emerging from The Poetry School and from the wider context of poetry's contemporary audience.

Unlike most anthologies of new voices, *Entering the Tapestry* contains voices familiar to us from courses, workshops and seminars we have led. In some cases, we have watched their poems develop, in others, found gems we didn't know were there. Whether a poem is ever finished or not is debatable, but we did look for poems that were close to the finishing line; that delighted us with humour and grace, formal agility and emotional power; poems that had found their speaker, who might have been looking elsewhere.

The variety of tone, style and diction reflects the distinctiveness of each voice and also, we like to think, the openness of The Poetry School and our wish not to impose a house style but to encourage individual expression. What is *not* there is also significant: poems fed on short rations of irony or fortified by anecdotal wit, cleverness for its own sake or poems betrayed by their anxiety to look contemporary. Instead, we have gone for something with a warmer spirit, more human and more generous. And we were surprised by how easily the poems bled into each other: the loss of one sister answered by another; two grandfathers sitting side by side; a piece of music echoed by another which seemed to have heard it; funeral upon funeral; and the public world lodged in the lyrical. Few people read poetry books from cover to cover but, while the individual poems in *Entering the Tapestry* encourage you to dip in, their relationships also invite you to follow the poems reaching out, touching fingertips and extending a continuum.

MIMI KHALVATI
GRAHAM FAWCETT

I

Anne Ryland

SEA SCRIPT

One vast page ranging away from view,
    no paragraphs for pauses. Where to begin,
how to find a loose thread that invites
    unravelling. Each sentence slips out of
its predecessor and into the next, wave
    upon wave of calligraphy, not a lapse or
hesitation in sight. This is a complex
    and perfect grammar, and I always loved
a verb table, the way tenses string
    together as pearls, each mirroring another,
and those cupboards a linguist builds
    in her mind, where accusative, dative,
genitive are stored for instant access,
    the carved drawers of etymology, where
tide derives from *time*. Later, I may
    evolve into marine lexicographer, a creature
of the shore, gathering and annexing
    the sea's textures, until I become bilingual
in its liquid language. But for now
    I must learn the words as a child does,
like braille, tracing them by finger
    in the sand, the slow kinaesthetic method.
My first letter is the shape of a small
    purse, or is it a lip, just slightly open.

Anne Ryland

On breaking through the skin of that old dream
where I resit my maths exam, I remember
the sister I never had. We chose her name,
conceived from her from a dictionary. Catriona.

A girl born under the potent spell of numbers,
so when she'd counted bottles on a shelf
she'd write the sums all over her pyjamas,
then trot contentedly into night, with proof

that life added up. I picture her aglow
at thirty, beguiled by probability.
She floods her senses in the Poisson Law
of Distribution, tastes the poetry,

each sister guarding her end of the sofa
while integers and images spark together.

Anna Robinson

FULL MOON

The night my mum kidnapped the local council,
locking them in the back of the Seven Feathers
Community Centre, we – me and my little sister Abigail –
stayed at home, with our babysitter Ann-Marie,

only we weren't babies and that night was a full moon.
Ann-Marie said we shouldn't look, so we did,
then she said especially not through glass, so my sister
ran into the kitchen and got every glass.

We looked at the moon through tumblers, wine stems,
a thick-bottomed tot glass, a brandy bowl etched
with the name Loretta, we added cracks and chips
to the craters and rilles, split the moon into eight

perfect little baby moons with the bubbled bottom
of a whisky glass, but best was when we broke
rocks on the surface with a rippled water glass,
blew it to bits, making a diamond of stars,

bright as birthmarks, that stretched across
the whole night. Meanwhile, Ann-Marie
was shouting – *Don't!* and *your mum'll kill you*,
or so I'd imagine, we were too busy. All I know

is by the time my mum set the council free
and came home, Ann-Marie was crying
saying what terrible children we were
and how she'd never come near us again.

Anna Robinson

DAYS LIKE THIS

We're running, heads thrown back so we can see
how fast we are, faster than the clouds
(today's windy) and faster than the police
whose cordon we broke through at Waterloo.

There's so many of us and the sun is hanging
so low above York Road and is bouncing itself
off so many windows it has made a long
gold tunnel that none of us could resist.

I have the megaphone. This is not normal.
I'm usually the one with the banner,
wind-surfing to rallies with someone smaller
than me, but not today – today I can see

my long voice spreading out in front
shimmering like a heat haze towards
the bridge where it blends with others
and we look like one, we believe we can fly.

We're heading for Westminster Bridge and later,
after the stand-off and riot (which will begin
when some drift home and the crowd gets smaller
and we're stuck and night's wet blanket takes

the shine off our skins, just before that woman
from Tottenham – Maria, I think – has her leg
broken by a police horse) will it prove
worth it? We won't get to win this one,

but we ran, heads back, down that road and now
on days like this, in a certain light, I'm weightless.

Anna Robinson

SHE'S OUT

They turn me out, with my torn velvet coat *Go alone,*
they say, *stand under that street lamp, breathe fog.*

They turn me out of the police station
through the double doors and into the dark.

But, as the outer door is opened and the fog
licks in to get me, I hear a sound – like a rush

of blood – it's cheering, there's people here,
maybe hundreds, waiting for me – their warm

hands reaching out, their eyes searching
with *Okay? Did they hurt you?* and *Now*

everything will be alright and I go the gauntlet
of warm hands all the way to the pub where a drink

is waiting. But, my beautiful coat is torn
and despite their heat I'm still shivering

and now, looking back I think it's because I knew
that when each of them needs me I might not be there,

I might not be able to, I might not know.

Anna Robinson

TOSHER

The sewer-hunters were formerly, and indeed are still, called by the name of
'Toshers', the articles which they pick up in the course of their wanderings
. . . being known among themselves by the general name of 'tosh', a word
more particularly applied by them to anything made of copper.

Henry Mayhew

A small brown door appears in the river wall
and this time she's through, passing along a tunnel
of strong brick till she comes to another door

made of iron, top-hinged and hanging; so to get
past you must push; and a man's voice says *Push*
if you must, push 'ard, but don't let 'em see you.

Tired of peace, she pushes the door and is hurled
against wall; momentarily blinded, gagged by a rush
of wind going the opposite way. She sees

the man in the half-light she's let in. His hat
is brown and old and that's all she could tell you
'cause of course she's scared, who knows what

will happen. He approaches. *Take these; you'll be*
needin'em. Hands her a canvas apron, a darkened
lantern which he straps to her chest, a bag and

a long hoe. He shows her how to cast light –
both ahead and below; to watch for rats
who may travel in gangs; *Show 'em respect,*

but niver fear and take not more'n they allow,
to block her light below grating or by the shore –
You must niver be seen helse you'll 'ave to cut

your lucky and then you couldn't come back,
not niver. He shows her all the uses of the hoe;
how to test the ground, rake mud, save herself.

He says *Listen for water, watch the tides,*
follow your nose – if you find your whack
you'll niver mind 'ow the wind blows for the rest

of your life. Then lastly, *Rule number one 'Niver*
travel halone' – 'ceptin' as you 'ave no choice.
He's gone. It's so dark. She flicks open

the shade of her lantern, lighting the tunnel ahead
a few feet, revealing archways of smaller tunnels
branching off the Main to somewhere she

must go. But which? To where? How will she know?
She follows her nose until – a familiar smell,
rosemary or pine, floats by and she follows till

the whisper of something like a voice stops her.
Rope and bone, rope and bone, you're not
alone, you're not alone. This she takes

as a sign and turns East below Narrow Wall.
The whisper persists. Her feet are damp and slimy.
Where is the tide? she thinks, *I was promised water.*

Her lantern flickers, she takes out the candle,
places it on the hoe and holds it out into
the distance; when it comes back still alight

she knows that the air at least is safe but still
her breath is laboured, she moves more slowly,
heavy now, eyes wider than the flame,

so it's only now that she sees – though it's been there
for ages – a copper throne threaded with silver,
too solid, too heavy for Toshers to take, rising

out of the brickwork to almost the ceiling and as she
approaches she raises her hands as if in prayer
and then her eyes, which are met by two small eyes,

rat eyes, and though startled she's neither surprised
nor afraid and the rat says *Welcome to our little*
lurk, rest awhile, you're in lavender now.

He invites her to sit, then sits beside her, claps
his hands and a thousand rats emerge from
the dark, scurrying, swarming around her throne

and as each passes her feet it leaves something
for her: old coins, nails, ropes, bones,
and each, after giving, licks her dirty feet

and passes to the back of the throng. She thanks
each one very much, admires each gift,
then the King, who is beside her, says

Good Toshers who don't flam get treated nice
down here. But, don't you be a dollymop;
each ding, each gift is a lesson, take them away,

study hard. Learn them by touch, smell,
whatever; but learn their value. We are family,
you must find your way back. Don't be a stranger!

He crowns her with a rusty tiara and the rats
cheer and everyone sings a song about love
and when it's over they disappear and then

she hears it – the roar of fast water, crashing
through tunnels but which, where? She runs back
the way she hopes she came, clutching her bag,

gripping the hoe, but the water is faster. She looks
back and sees it – this giant white fist
filling the tunnel, and she's down, and drowning

in too many thoughts when as soon as she knows it
she's swept out of the tunnel, out of The Main, and then
with one push through the hanging gate, where the water

calms down, rocks her awhile before a hiccup
spits her through the old brown door, back
onto the beach, and though the beach is warm

and as gold as a story, she doesn't stay, she picks
up her bag, lantern and hoe and looks for her shoes
which she finds, right by the pier where she'd left them.

BELLS

Five minutes after he'd left to play darts
she sent me after him
for half a bottle of whiskey.
When I caught up with him he told me to wait
disappearing through the double doors
into the surge of warmth and orange light.
Minutes later he returned with the bottle
warning me to hurry back and not fall.
I ran home with the unwrapped bottle
and sat rock-still on the couch with my sisters
while she drank from a mug.
She didn't like to be disturbed while drinking
reminding her of all the stuff
she'd landed herself with,
five kids and none of us boys.
She slumped forward twisting her fingers
and tugging at her lips till we could
see her teeth and pale bloodless gums.
All the time she smoked
lighting each cigarette with the stub in her hand
holding long conversations with spies
my dad and Elizabeth Taylor had paid to plague her,
stabbing her nicotine finger in their faces.

Frances Angela

GRANDFATHER

By the river
a man was sitting on a bench talking
to a woman. He looked like my grandfather.
I could hear their conversation.
She had been to her niece's wedding
and drank champagne.
He listened politely, his dusty silver hair
nebulous against his navy blue scarf.
After some time the woman rose to leave and he
sat on alone watching a passing boat.
I felt an impulse to join him
not necessarily to talk, but to sit in the silence
of my childhood.

Ruth Smith

MY GRANDFATHER'S MAGNIFYING GLASS

When the papers came
he could make news jump
in its thick chrome rim,
keeping a set distance
from what thronged there.
Some days he'd sleuth
through dark green paperbacks
or study form, reckoning
the odds until the figures
doubled – then his glass
would droop, slip sideways
from his lap and land
at his feet, a scoop of light.

I'd pick it up and magnify
my lifeline, close in
on finger-whorls, find pillars
sprouting from my hands.
Once and once only, I peered
into his hog-bristling ears,
misting the lens as I moved
section by section across
the moonscape of his skin,
a slow reconnaissance
of trackways, wadis, folds,
his cleft frown – and shrieked
at the fierce, brown eye
that was within an inch of mine.

Ruth Smith

A HALO AS BIG AS THE SUN

After the bible story
and the wheeze and pedal-clack
of the harmonium
we'd sit at a table,
sharing a box of crayons,
to draw pictures of Jesus.

Christmas was babe-in-a-basket
– a single tinfoil star
and during the year some of us
traced a tall cerulean saint,
one hand upraised,
and a halo as big as the sun
we'd already coloured in.

At Easter we needed green
for our high, domed hills
with their rickety crosses
and someone used all the red
to daub a hanging man
whose whole weight fell
from arms that measured

the paper with their fingertips.
When we went to museums
we got to know his owlish face
from Byzantine mosaics
and liked the colours, the silvers and golds
in their shining cubes. In time,
we'd recognise him anywhere

for he attracted light. His hair
was full of it — and his clothes.
We'd find him blazoned
in churches, washed onto walls;
hung in the Kunstmuseum,
the Prado, the Louvre and see him
again and again

as a bloated child
at a stiff madonna's breast;
barefoot in a Tuscan landscape
with clear, light flesh
and perfect musculature,
or haggard — arching
a tense, tormented frame
with soldiers below and every rib drawn in.

Robert Chandler

ELENA

If your sister mentions your name, what I hear is always a story
you told us that evening,

The story of how, after you had moved to Tashkent – Russian
father, American mother, and you were born in China,

And in 1956 you had all gone back to the USSR, what with
your father suffering *toskà* for the motherland

And your sister, Nadezhda, meaning 'Hope', dreaming she could
contribute, with her knowledge of languages,

To international understanding – what I hear is how, in Tashkent,
a city your grandfather, General Bitov,

Had once conquered for Tsar Nikolay but where you now all
lived in one room, since your holy fool of a father

Had entrusted to GosBank all the dollars he had saved during
thirty years reluctantly trading timber,

And where you were trapped, since the USSR, then as ever, was
easier to get into than out of,

And the only blessing was that the Russian Consul in Tsientsyn
had had the grace to dissuade your father,

Playing on his worries over baby Misha's asthma, and the cold,
and the journey, from returning before Stalin's death,

In which case you would all have been shot, or scattered around
the Gulag – yes, what I hear is how, in Tashkent,

Your mother once boiled some valerian root to tide you over
who knows what upset, and while it was cooling,

The liquid was drunk by the cat, who then slipped into the cup-
board containing precious teacups from China,

Your family's last link with a world now lost for ever, and the cat,
crazed by the valerian,

Was unable to find its way out of the cupboard and began to
charge round in circles, pulverising the china

And so aggravating its panic, which made it charge faster, weav-
ing together this story I always remember you by.

Robert Chandler

DIMA

There's a book to be written, I said, about how people responded
to the news that Stalin had died – and Dima told me how

He himself had been six, and had burst into tears, and his moth-
er, not daring to scold him or (God forbid!) give vent to her joy,

Had firmly told him to go and tidy the mess he'd made in the
kitchen, and Dima did as he was told but then, soon afterwards,

Their gigantic cat contrived to inextricably wedge himself behind
their ever-so-sturdy Soviet radiator,

And from this place of confinement the cat began to orchestrate
the most satanic of screeches and yowls which might –

So Dima's parents feared – have enraged their malevolent neigh-
bours, or even inspired them,

Hungry for living space as neighbours so often tended to be, to
write a denunciation, accusing the family of who knows what

Blasphemous rituals on this most tragic of days, when tens of
millions had been suddenly orphaned –

And so, since cat and radiator were equally unmovable, and it was impossible to acquire the necessary tools

Except by calling a plumber, they had called their plumber, a lover of vodka, who was finally carried

Into their flat late in the evening, far away in the world of spirit and unable to wield the tools of his trade

Which, however, he had at least (thank God!) remembered to bring with him – and so drunken Ivan had lain in state on the floor

And issued instructions to Dima's father, who succeeded in moving the radiator and thus liberating

The exhausted beast, who – as I only now realize – must have been infected with at least a small dose of the hysteria

That had nearly the whole population of the Union of Soviet Socialist Republics in its tightening grip

And would soon cause hundreds of men, women and children to be trampled to death as they wedged themselves into Red Square on their way to pay their respects to the corpse of the Father of Peoples.

Valerie Clarke

(From the Hayward Gallery's Exhibition 'Spectacular Bodies')

JAN WANDELAAR — DRAWING OF A SKELETON, EARLY 18TH
CENTURY

Omens there were,
owls,
a dog howling,
clouds spilling the moon.

The garden, so like the one
in my painting,
yet unlike.

I hadn't sketched the house,
just trees split by a path
like a silver necklace,
a few cracked slabs,
steps,
up which something left undrawn

climbed steadily upwards.

Valerie Clarke

(from 'Spectacular Bodies')

G. B. MANFREDINI — FEMALE BUST WITH OPEN ABDOMEN.
TERRACOTTA 1773–76

How elegantly the young matron
    lifts flaps of skin
from the artichoke of her womb.

How neatly the small intestine
    is packed behind rib-cage
in pink-looped butchers' sausages.

A robe slips from her shoulders
    baring dark copper nipples.
Below carefully dressed hair,

her brows are puzzled. She prays –
    I am clay in his hands
as I was in my husband's.

But the artist is tender,
    moulding a flower in the
peeled back flesh of each groin.

Valerie Clarke

AFTER HEARING A CD OF THE LAST CASTRATO SINGER IN
THE SISTINE CHAPEL CHOIR★

Seeming to live somewhere else,
the stepped garden a route to it,

I stand out of doors. It's barely light,
still snowing, frost rasping indoor skin.

My fingers blanch when I stroke
mahonias' freezing flowers.

For a while there's silence, then
the two small boys next door erupt

in an orgy of noise. A snowball lands
at my feet with a soft flummox.

By now I'm truly cold. What idiot
maps new worlds without coat or gloves,

surveys the ice-ringed patio in slippers?
The Arctic is a state of mind

open to anyone. And you Alessandro,
how did you feel when you sang?

★Alessandro Moreschi (1858–1922), recorded 1902, 1904

33

II

Julia Lewis

TREES: A SEASONAL SEQUENCE

I
Red. For example the cherry
  prunus avium
in a patch of civic ground or suburban front garden; part of the
  blossom festival,
dawdling through passably anonymous summers. Whose
  gossipy leaves
will quieten in autumn, limp elliptical firedrops
  that hang
on a vertical axis (without wind, as though weighted). Its branches
  extend
to curve up like loop-fringed arms on a long sung note. If a breeze
  should disconnect
a leaf it seems arbitrary – they'll all go together when the tree thinks
  now
as though hold and relax of the hold were
  an act
of musculature. In fact, leaves are shrugged off with
  corklike callouses,
cell-barricades at the leafstalk. Hundreds of mouthlets
  gape red, slacken;
daunted, as though before railings, by lack of admission.
  Abscission. Sap
gated; each leaf placed outside the enclosure. Cold
  turns the keys.
The whole Order of winter trees resumes fasting
  and abstinence.

II

Silver. Thick–muscled, fissured roots
like limbs, almost level
with human eyes, of heaved–up
or sinking elephants

plunged knuckle-, knee-,
or shoulder–deep in a steep
English daffodil bank.
Old beeches. Watchers

of a square stone house
with rained–on eaves
warmed from within
by light.

A traveller's horseshoes
might slow here, for
it is February, the daffodils
not yet out in the verges

to strike Spring fire
from the hooves,
and February's purpose
uncertain as rain–light.

Indoors, perhaps steam
and a child sat reading
as rain–troop rattles
attack and recede

over the gutter's quiet
glops and gloops.
Meanwhile these watchmen
never challenge.

They let and are let to be;
majesty evoking majesty.
Their sodden skin,
in places shrunk, in others

sagging, a mark of what
is available, neutral,
to one who stands guard,
skeleton by the gate.

To greet them
with outstretched arm
and palm cupped
brotherly, reassuring,

around their humped watchfulness –
at the same time to watch, yourself,
how they dry their vast crowns
under hanging skies

you may feel the fine rain
fall the length
of the funnel
of your upturned nostril.

III
Green. Nature's verticality

– having sped from seed
   balanced itself with a few side-strokes

become nature's sketch

– though not spared the bureaucracy of forming needles.

★

The monotony,

the extreme standing-up,
of the log road to heaven.

Ants form a dual carriageway.

★

Lower rungs

(within reach of goblin fingers)
clogged; their long pale dishcloths

belong to the kingdom of roots.

★

Larchbone of my spine!

– an arrowhead loosed toward puberty
   bearing a mouth that gasped 'Wait'!

to the zinging wind & piles of unwashed dishes

★

Larch fronds. Oh, new

spring green on timeless summer blue,
to lie horizontal under your spars

& learn to swim the sky with you,
paddling the emptied pink gloves of my palms

★

until the stars glitter on the draining-board of the dark.

Julia Lewis

THE MIRACLE

Remember that fantastic spider's web?
Fantastic less as feature than as feat
of structural engineering that had stretched
the top thread, measuring some ten metres,
from one tip of our neighbour's pampas grass
to a branch halfway up our almond tree.
An invisible drawbridge spanned the twin front paths.
Its height gave clearance: we passed underneath
a miracle, just going in and out of doors.
The web hung where steps started and paths stopped.
Lack of disturbance meant it had the chance
to grow huge and round, like a firework, or
a station clock, and grant us love's whole sequence:
discovery, unforeseen endurance, shock.

Julia Lewis

MOON IN A BLANKET

The only copy I have of Debussy's *Clair de lune* is the one I played from when I was fourteen, the one my father bought as a young man before I was born, though he swore he was never able to get past the first two pages. Now those pages are all nicotine-brown with age, their centre-folds split and the edges limp, dog-eared and torn in a hundred places, impossible to turn without help. Why is French music printed on such big paper? A Jean Jobert Paris edition folded in a United Music Publishers cover, it has the number 100 written on the front in my father's careful handwriting (his collection was meticulously indexed) and reminds me thirty years later that I never asked his permission to have it on permanent loan.

I suppose it isn't surprising that the pieces I chose to learn myself took on a vivid life in my imagination which the pieces my teacher gave me to learn rarely did. In most cases they all retain for me something of their original aura of private magic or public duty. But in this case the piece's magical aura is fainter, veneered with the curious blankness of guilt. For some reason I took a dislike to Debussy in my later teens from which I've never quite recovered. I think it arose partly in response to a Christmas present called *Lives of the Great Composers*: a hefty volume from which I received the impression that Debussy treated his mother callously in her declining years. I disliked his face, too, it put me in mind of the character of Komerovsky in *Doctor Zhivago*. These slight indications, together with a film of Nijinsky's life which represented the dancer masturbating on stage to *L'après-midi d'un faune*, combined to convince me that French Impressionism was decadent with its cool, deliberated sensuality. From then on I blocked my ears against seduction by mists of clustered ninths.

Julia Lewis

THE ART OF TIMING

When I started to learn Debussy's *Clair de lune*, the five flats of the key signature presented a negligible difficulty in comparison with the troubling 9/8 time signature which was completely unfamiliar and made no sense to me at all. I think my father must have demonstrated the opening bars and I began by copying what I remembered. At the 'tempo rubato', however, a pulse began to communicate itself via the chordal progression, rendering an intellectual understanding of the triple beat less necessary, and once the continuous semiquavers began they led me in complete confidence almost to the end – one had only to keep them going. By the time I took the piece to my teacher I knew the notes, and must have sounded as though I understood the rhythm, too, for it didn't occur to him to explain it.

But neither did it occur to me to ask. Perhaps this is the real reason the piece troubles me: it's imbued with the sense that in certain moods seems to characterise the whole of my childhood – that life's endless mysteries and difficulties were automatically as insurmountable as they were incommunicable. Incommunicable, that is, to myself – I'm not sure I could have formulated the concepts of asking for help or explanation without help or explanation. However, I strove to appear competent, and in this case succeeded completely by winning for the first time my class and the under-16s' cup in our local music festival. And so it came about that I sat in the front row of the hall, wearing a daringly fashionable pair of blue patent-leather shoes with four-inch heels, next to the other prizewinners, for the prize-giving recital.

When it came to my turn to play I heard the adjudicator stand up to comment that in his opinion 'this is how the piece *should* be played.'

I wasn't sure whether that meant I had deviated from a conventional reading, nor did I know how I could duplicate a previous performance. On my way to the platform the click of my heels on the parquet seemed to draw extra attention to my shoes in the silence. Next I had to pass the festival's lady administrator. Every year since I was quite small I had crept by her as she checked her typed list on a little baize-covered table by the stairs leading up to the stage, but she had never acknowledged me before. This lady now beamed at me. The effect on me of all this affirmation was mixed, given my conviction that I had only a vague idea of what I was supposed to be doing.

Next comes arranging the music on the stand, dog-earing the turns, palms clammy. The spotlight feels too low, and turning the piano-stool knobs in full view of an audience is an extreme form of penance, for it is always an experiment which way is up and which down, like the mushroom in *Alice*, and in my anxiety to appear professional about it, and if the knobs are stiff, I can almost sprain my wrists. Then those crazy blue patent-leather heels! It was one of the occasions I wished I'd had a fussy, controlling type of mother. I'd never realised how much my legs and feet trembled when I was nervous, and now when I sat on the stool and tested the depth of the sustaining pedal, my right heel, as I transferred weight to my toes, reverberated like a woodpecker against the polished wood. I ground my heel as hard as I could into the floor, and settled my hands on the keys.

In the placement of those three crucial opening thirds I had become familiar with a particular sensation, as though I was a pilot with a mission to hit – perhaps with sandbags rather than bombs – three targets in a row whilst leaving the whole of the rest of the city sound asleep. It was a kind of terrorised calm in which the only course of action was to abandon my fingers to some beneficent influence I didn't, but wished I could, trust. I had no inkling that the piece I had chosen was by its very nature acutely responsive to the approach I felt so anxious about.

Tony McKeown

SHE PLAYS A LULLABY

She plays a lullaby
on the piano
– the little girl above –
over and over and
starting again, each time
off-kilter in a different
place.

At difficult moments
her fingers falter,
then speed up
at her favourite points
played with too much
feeling

like these memories
I keep replaying.

Tony McKeown

THOUGH I HAVE NOT WRITTEN

I am here. As the grey heron is here,
hunched over and staring intently

into the blank page of the water.
If you get too close, he flies

to the other side of the loch
with a call like the crack of a whip.

Heather Coffey

THE WATER COMMON

Pub talk is of stand-pipes,
the shedding of yellow leaves
only halfway to autumn.

Rain, rain, like a hymn,
my days spent skywatching
for the one grey cloud

which flies away at once
over the uncut furze.
The heath crackles underfoot,

tinder about to spark.
Dust haunts my bare legs,
water an aspiration,

a growing desire in me
to spring like a rose, dewy
and open-eyed and new,

to wreathe my limbs
in the song of water,
a nightly fix of it

by the fence, listening
to an illicit hiss,
a neighbour's sprinkler set on low,

to be one of his lettuces,
even in a frame,
letting water crawl all over me.

Mary MacRae

LAUNDRY

1

Low tide, high wind; sailboarders and clouds
slip across horizontals, slice air
to bright untied ribbons which stream out
behind a girl with unplaited hair

who's running by the edge of the sea
where colour threads through light, like satin
ruffling a frill at neckline or sleeve,

and bunched wave-tips of creamy linen
fall crumpled on shore. When I think *fresh*
it smells like this, the water as green
as a bar of Sunlight soap, washing

me back to a small house, a Monday,
you and me alone in the kitchen
in the half-sweet, damp scent of laundry.

2

On the gas stove there's a fizzy brew
of whites in a large tub. You poke them
with a dolly stick, add Reckitt's Blue
in its little bag through clouds of steam

then plunge blindly through the thick lather
with long wooden tongs, spattering foam.
Rinsing is an up and down matter,

red fists jumping and diving like fish
in swirls of bleached slow-motion seaweed.
You dry your fingers gently; I wish
they weren't so cracked and sore, their creases

split apart. You let me help glue them
together with Nu-skin; your hands feel
rough as the kitchen towel, and as warm.

3
All this air's gone to my head; leaning
into the salt gale I watch the sea
ruffle its green, and it's like looking
straight down into that small room, as real

and clear as a bar of soap that's caught
the light. We still sit there, drinking tea,
you with a Woodbine, and talk and talk;

we never dry up. I see you comb
my hair into scrawny plaits, then find
freshly ironed blue ribbons to tie them:
two figures, spotlit by a window,

bright as glass. But although I'm listening,
what with the boom of water and wind,
I can't hear a word you're saying.

Mary MacRae

LIFE STORY

Night, and you step out into blackness, over
the side of the silent vessel, dreading that you
or your boots might slip and miss the rung, one
false move your last. Between above and below
you hang breathless, locked into history –
and this is what you chose, what you want.

No moon, no stars – though light's not what you want –
only a sound like a thumb rubbing over
corrugated card as the men in your story
run down the ladder, loaded with kit. And you
feel rather than see, where the man below
you wavers, shifts his pack, now there's no-one.

'Dropped like a stone,' I hear you say, 'just one
splash and he'd gone.' A small smile. You want
to cry, can't quite believe the man below
the water wasn't you, rehearse it over
and over again to convince yourself that you
survived the war, came home to tell your story.

It comes back to me now: hearing your story
I saw what you saw, clear as glass, how someone
plummeted down, but whether it was you,
or him, or someone else, I didn't want
to know. Slid through a door that closed over
his head, from dark above to dark below.

Whoever that man was who plunged below,
if you're the secret sharer of his story
then I'm yours. And the story isn't over;
when you dropped like a stone you left me one
part short, however much I wanted – want –
to understand the plot and why I miss you.

Taller than life, younger than in death, you
come to visit me now from way below
the spirit-level of dream; won't speak. I want
to ask if you can love me – that old story –
but don't; put my arms around you one
last time and say, I love you, over and over.

I conjured you from below by telling your story
and then I saw our two stories are one:
can I want yours to end before mine's over?

Mary MacRae

VISITANTS

Each time it's like starting afresh:
a day full of mist and promise, trees heavy
with wet, the silver birches ghostly,

revenants in the soft air,
all movement slow, as if gravity
were too much to carry

and rain falling on leaves,
tapping weightlessly,
no after-shock, no resonance,

only repeated patterns of sound
like speech in a language
we might at any moment understand

or owls that call in the dark
for an answer, all their energy
spent in growing, in making . . .

To be part of the wave breaking –
the way water runs off a rock
when the sea's drawn forward

and pours itself over hump-backed granite,
glazing it, then rolls back, carrying
a white stone at its centre, an inner eye –

is to pass through an invisible skin
to the solid core, slipping
over its smoothness

to be received again
into the rhythm of swaying waters,
their green depths.

We start where wind is visible,
sea-currents in the narrows joining and parting
in treacly swirls and clashes

while skylarks sing non-stop
in white noise – but more golden,
like wine being poured into a glass –

when suddenly, across the hot shimmer of ferns –
horses, thirty or forty of them
massed against a backdrop of sea and sky,

bright-coloured, waiting, expectant,
as if they'd been there from the start,
somewhere we could only half recall.

Why had they picked their way along
this winding path, stepping with delicate hooves
between heather and the coiled roots of blueberry

right to the peak, small heaps of dried dung
marking their route, and stood,
face-on to the wind, looking out?

Nothing to graze on; just rock this close
to the edge, and a few flowers – scabious,
campion, tormentil, lodged in the cracks.

They must have gazed into a space
so blank, so unfocused in its melding
of blue-green and blue,

it was as if they were inside it,
part of the light that pulled the sea's thread,
of an expanse we could only long for.

In their bright stillness they seemed
like pictures from a child's story-book,
larger than life, fabulous.

To them we were no more than rocks
or trees to brush past, neutral,
but they made me afraid;

I couldn't walk among them,
push past their warm flanks,
feel their breathing, the deep-veined necks.

As they move on together,
mares and foals pressed close, they seem
to carry with them a kind of darkness

as if we'd looked too near the sun –
small plants, birds, stones, all alive in the dark –
and I thought of the mares giving birth,

how their tissues would soften and dilate
so the young could be pushed into the light,
and how close unfold is to enfold.

We watch them go, trotting easily
over the stony ground, their haunches
curved like centaurs', the stallions

edgy, uneasy, until they come to rest
in a field high above the sea, magnified
in the clear light, separate.

One bird sings from a golden bush;
a single-voiced bird announcing
a small breaking-through,

an invisible mechanism
of oiled levers falling
to close, to open.

Deborah Sacks

After 'The Wild Swans' by Hans Christian Andersen

I wear my hands like thimbles; numb to them,
To all else but them. My hands themselves
Are nettles, needling, white budded,
Grown where my hands used to be.
I am less than the least servant girl
Who has a clean dress and a dry bed.
I keep to myself, go when I may
Meet no one, by waysides and wastelands.
I know where the nettles grow wide and waist high.
I waste neither nettles nor daylight. The dampness
Is inside of me; I cough like a crow.
My thoughts marshal me like armies of green
Daggers. I am called a madwoman and a witch.
But it is a saneness to me, this task which has its own dictates
And seasons, which is itself a world: all green.
I have shed tears to cry, 'I am not made
For this', but my nimble fingers answer,
'You are'. So my pity grows as after rain.
The days whiten. I know the pain
Is time which must be lived. My brothers'
Feathers whiten. I will throw these shirts
As I would my arms around their necks.
It is a strange homecoming, this coming into
Oneself, this disinheritance.

Jacqueline Gabbitas

THE PASSAGE

At my window watching city rain slant off the passage wall,
all I can think is: *This is the passage back home.*

On two or three seasonless nights a vast moon
fills our narrow, red-walled path with such
a glorious white light I'm forced to stand holding
the green wooden gate (taller than me even now) in one
shaking hand while the other fixes me to the gatepost.

You'd think I'd become invisible, a shaft of light,
but I'm just very clear in the details of my white skin,
my hair, my clothes; the third nail on my left hand's
ripped to the quick, a stud on my cuff is broken like
a dropped-off bit of star, my shoes need re-soling.

You'd think I'd be blinded or made deaf by such
roaring light but when I look down my heart is
beating like a mouse's through my chest and I hear
the out-breaths of every half-sleeping sparrow.
Each of these things brings me closer to the garden.

Bed after bed of beans, peas and potatoes and then
the compost heap and with it the Long-tailed 'uns.
– I've only ever seen one: a bit of greasy chicken skin
in her mouth, her paws, weedy, fastened on a plank.
When she shot off she made out she'd never seen me.

This is a nest, but it's not hers. I crouch down against
the washing-line post. I won't take my eyes off the heap.
Like in the passage, the moon fills our garden with white.
And in the house behind me, people I love get ready for bed:
lights switch off and on and off again. Here the heap moves.

First, potato peelings slip down then egg-shells roll,
crack, crunch against my shoes. But they don't emerge,
the rats, one by one: whisker, nose, paw. They come out in pairs
and they're quick. They don't swarm, but they are organised,
each pair assigned to finding scraps of rotting food.

This is how still and clear the night is: not one rat
has stopped, perched on its haunches and sniffed the air
in order to catch me out. I'm just a bulky shadow – inert.
I watch the activity: one rat disappears with bits of beef,
rotten eggs, it reappears. Another does the same.

Apple skins, bananas, sour chitterlings all get dragged
into the heap. My neck will ache for days but I daren't move.
The vast moon, higher than ever, is now so small the garden
and passage are totally black. The rats are hidden in the heap.
In the house behind me, doors are dark and unlocked.

My shoulders, elbows, are stiffer than I thought they'd be,
stiffer even than my neck, my knees. I smell of muck
from the onion beds, muck and onions and wet dog.
But I'm here, still held by the moonlight I saw and the way
the rats worked: quietly, quickly, undisturbed.

Jacqueline Gabbitas

ME, HOLDING YOUR HAND

Eyup, June, d'you remember Big Tessie
slouched on my Mam's dressing table?
Her porcelain fingers all shiny and fat?
And her eyeholes? Remember
those black eyeholes?
No, the eyes were in a tin in the kitchen cupboard.
Button tin. Silver Jubilee biscuits.
Mam kept them there after you pushed them out.
Tessie's eyes – storm-grey and large
like ours – kept safe all these years in a biscuit tin.
God, she scared me that doll but, even eyeless,
she had something.

June? June, d'you know your eyes are open?

Slouched by the mirror she was,
like Siamese twins in those antique
medical freak books my Dad picked up.
God she was cold, and her lips?
– it seemed odd, to me,
how you could see her front teeth.

I know they've ripped your mouth, June,
to get that tube in. There's blood
on your lips,
drying round words,
round white plastic.

Remember her face? White with fat,
rosy cheeks, rosy lips?
If I kissed you (like I want to, daren't),
what I'd taste is me in you.
I can't think what you can taste,
except maybe painkillers, blood.

Remember her fingers? China like her face
shiny and fat. Creamy.
No nail varnish. Nails clean.
When they brought you in
was there scum under your fingernails
from mopping up your own sick?
I think of stroking your fingers,
holding your hand, but if I do
(like I want to, daren't), I know
I'll knock the needle out.

June, can you hear me?
I've brought you a book. Paddington Bear.

There's dried blood everywhere,
on the sheets, your face, under your nails.
I want to clean it up but I don't know how.
They tell us it's bad. I want to put your fingers
in my mouth, make your blood warm, clean.

I should wipe that spit off your chin
before they give you more adrenaline.
– Afterwards, Mam remembers the bloating,
the steroids. Me? I saw what the adrenaline did.

Remember that rag doll we tipped
up to say Maa-ma and laugh?
Tessie wasn't that kind of doll.

They've already tipped you up once, June,
shifted the whole bed
to keep your heart from stopping
– we got sent out the ward.

And when your heart stops again that's that.
None of this drama; no beeps; no Bach:
just silent monitors and pulling out cables;
just all of us crying and me
holding your hand June, thinking how cold it is.

Lucy Hamilton

AFTER THE MARKET, VALLAURIS

Men dismantle metal frames
    skilful as children
unlocking the steel limbs
    of a giant meccano;
the refuse truck arrives
    with mechanical lift;
pigeons strut and flap
    in the clatter and banging.

The afternoon hush
    of French lunch-time,
cool behind shutters
    or languid in cafés,
lulled by the plane trees' rustling
    palmate leaves, trunks
and boughs white as bones
    dappled with grey.

A boy appears
    on a shiny bike,
dimpled knees pumping
    cellulite thighs,
circles and circles the square
    as if solitude's grabbed
him by the hand – out for
    a breath of fresh air.

And, as if believing himself
    invisible, an old man
shuffles across the square
    toward the fountain,
slowly removes each green
    jelly sandal to splash
under fresh water, then struggles
    to bend to fix the strap.

Later, as he shambles back
    and the little boy
cycles round and round
    and the young men shout,
the moment feels eternal
    as any old man's war,
any child's loneliness,
    any sister's slow dying.

Lucy Hamilton

SPHAGNUM *BATRACHOSPERMUM*

Its need for
  fresh water
and love of
  colour –
gradations
  of red
through violet
  to iridescent
blue-green –
  remind me
of my mother's
  fingers

shaping wreaths
  in wet
emerald moss
  and indigo
heathers,
  fleshing
wire frames
  into crosses
with her ringed
  hands and
pink, unlacquered
  nails –

and my sister's hair
   in threads
and filaments,
   the sheen
of droplets on
   her skin
make me think
   of bobbles
on a string,
   rosary beads,
the structure
   of blood.

Beverley Charles Rowe

THE PSALM OF THE OTICS

The otic blessed the birds and the children
By poking their bodies with a short stick.

The look of ecstasy on their faces
can hardly be imagined.

I love the otics.
Their goodness is a beacon in an evil world.

They walk naked into the light of god
and bathe in the beauty of his excellence.

Beverley Charles Rowe

LOVE AND THE OTIC

'This is the story of my day'
said the mayor,
as his eyes rested on the list
of winning candidates.

'I had not slept at all,
so my minds were misted
by a rain of fine particles,
each a wish.

'I focused on one and found
that I could speak all languages:
hate, joy, ridicule,
even the language of fear.

'I was aroused by a tender young otic,
smiling above her milkmaid dress.
Obligingly she bent over, skirt raised.
That was satisfactory.

'I flung a few shillings at her,
which caused some consternation,
even outrage. I never understood why.
These people often fail to speak clearly.'

THE OTICS' GARDEN

'Come and see our garden' said the otic,
leading me by the nose
through their living-room.

'If you'd come next week
all this would be concrete,'
he said.

He showed me gleefully
the lovebites that scar the lawn,
the passion that fertilises the dead lilac.

The lawn-mower has left smudges
on his back and skull;
the incinerator has singed his hairs.

He muttered 'These misshapen apple trees
are a metaphor for my anger,
because my heart has grown out of true.'

On a shady bank the knotweed
declines by the year but
the coriander walks riot in the spring.

'Why does my fig tree bear
only unripe fruit?'
he asked me with a narrow smile.

We went back into the living-room,
ready to see his friends and relations
wither and fade.

Beverley Charles Rowe

FLEEING IRAQ

The reeds we use to make music grow in a place my father showed me.

As my son and I finished our evening meal, the rice and fish that the women served us, I said 'Tomorrow we cut reeds to make pipes.'

He seemed to understand – I wasn't sure.

The women came to remove the food, to make a meal on what we left. I said to my daughter 'You come too.'

My son is soft, furry; my daughter lithe and smooth.

The reeds must be taken very early. It was hardly light when I cast off. I showed them which reeds were good and how to cut them.

The pipes we made lasted many weeks. My son was an eager player, my daughter more skilful. Their mother smiled and clapped when we played.

My son was burnt by the fire they dropped during the first raid but lived on until the third attack. This caught my daughter in the open. Her flesh peeled away, purple and burned hard. She did not live on.

Among these dry hills I hear only the sound of water flowing through reeds.

1996

Matt Barnard

In answer to the Jewish question I answer 'no'
though by my brow, my eyes, my nose you'd be forgiven
    for thinking so;

for even in a room of Jews on Sabbath Friday, one asked
if I was one and said, of all the men there, I was the one
    you wouldn't ask.

I followed their rituals, took water like proper Jews
do, like my father's mother's father must have done, but
    I watch the news

and see stone-throwers nightly face the tanks, and lies
and wonder who my lost people are who can only
    see one side, eye

for an eye, ten deaths for a death. Who is counterfeit,
those who lose their lands, their histories, or the lessons
    they beget?

Matt Barnard

THE BENDS

And let this be a lesson, frogmen,
to those who return too fast from a foreign element, the
        punishment
is terrible. Terrible for those like Icarus

who believe they've mastered the other place
with feathers glued to bamboo shoots, or prosthetic webbing.

Sojourners, be humble
as the earthworm is humble.

He embraces the earth, lets it pass through him, he burrows he eats
    his element,
blind, deaf, mute. He knows the vengeance of birds, their iron
        beaks.
So when you rise in a cacophony of bubbles

through the ocean's unmeasured mass,
come back slowly. Listen

to your breathing.
Think of the half-opened door of the moon, how it let slip
men into its bare pantry.

Of the tips of mountains and their time-lock on life,
and be thankful for yours.

Linda Black

BETWEEN FINGER AND THUMB

Think of the word *abracadabra* – now picture the hand movements: conjuring, coaxing – a slow pull backwards through thick air, as though grasping a fine but invisible thread tightly between finger and thumb. Or the pulling of a single hair with relish; a look of glee, a mask of evil. To achieve the desired effect the thread must, of course, be attached to something living, feeling, subjugated. Nothing sudden happens here – no yanking, no gross movements – all is in the stance, the poise of delivery, the very doing. Not that this *action*, this *doing* can be said to be in any way ponderous. The desire is measured; the extraction savoured. Of the persecutor, little is known.

Take this description, not of a drawing, but of the *memory* of a drawing executed some time ago, in pencil, in an exercise book, on unlined paper: A woman is walking along a street – of this I am sure, though no road, kerb or pavement is visible. She is wearing a winter coat, belted at the waist and a hat, possibly of wool – let us say she is well wrapped up. She is neither young, nor sinister. We approach her from the back. Trailing behind her, on a leash, are two hind legs, not animal, but human. The leash is held between finger and thumb. If it is not, it *ought* to be.

Linda Black

THE YELLOW CHAIR

Wasn't always, isn't really – underneath it is, as I remember it, a dark-ish blue, not quite petrel. Scanning the room I can't find a match and decline to lift its skirt. Three thoughts occur, vie for precedence. I like to be exact, attend to minutiae.

★

I am mistaken. A petrel is a sea bird, related to the shearwaters, typically flying far from land; the colour (though it isn't) is petrol blue.

★

Small crosses like sideways kisses are woven into the fabric, regularly, but how far apart I couldn't say – and dots, I believe there are dots. I could liken the pattern to swallows – there is something in the curve of a wing.

★

There are no arms. Its wide back curls around my shoulders, tapers like a cut-off triangle, to meet a circular seat. A further point – the springs have gone; under the cover I have placed – some time ago – an old feather cushion and several pieces of thickish card. They slip about sometimes.

★

Its legs are wooden, hidden. It is my grandmother's chair, a low chair, a feeding chair.

★

I do look later; about some things, I am completely wrong.

TANTIE DIABLESSE TEACHES US HOW TO MAKE PUNCH

one of sour
Use only limes. Lemons are inferior.
Collect the fruit, just ripened,
ready to be plucked. Cut,
squeeze dry, then sting your tongue
with the liquid. Savour the act
(the aftertaste should be washed linen).

two of sweet
This is the stage of soft brown
Januaries, when sea air brushes
bleached cane arrows: set these alight
to ruin breeze-white sheets.
Burnt honey, ground down to weep.
Cinnamon; cloves; cutlasses;
add one drop of bitters
and strained syrup goes in next.

three of strong
Gold rum, not white –
head for the darkness. Wrap
rust-blood chains around old oak,
with a cooper's touch. The air
should shimmer above
your measure
like rain on hot pitch.

four of weak
Journey's end: the fabric
that binds the whole.
Spread hummingbird baskets
on q*u'est-ce-qu'il-dit*? cloaks, then
choose apples (small, hard ones)
or king oranges, bursting with juice. And
always bear in mind, the flavour
is best when you crush
without pity.

Qu'est-ce-qu'il-dit or keskidee: a bird named after its call

Fawzia Kane

TANTIE DIABLESSE WAS IN LOVE, ONCE

He would make me call him *massa*,
sometimes in private, always in public.

At the end of his day's journey, I would
soothe his feet with copper water.

Once, in the dark, he confessed to me
that he too came from dirt and hunger.

I remained silent, remembering the warmth
of my mother's skin, milk-washed

and smooth. When he slept, I traced a line
with my finger, slowly, across his throat.

Fawzia Kane

Let me make it clear, this wasn't my fault.
She begged for my help, so I gave her
some bush-tea, like all the other times.
But suddenly she let go, and just went quiet.
Her eyes couldn't close.

They laid the child on her belly, then
it stopped breathing too.

When *he* got the news, he howled like a dog
at the moon. He even bent down with us
to put the two of them in the ground,
and had a master mason carve a tomb
from marble, imported from Italy.

To this day I can feel the calluses on her hand
when she grabbed me in pain.

I wasn't supposed to look into his eyes, much less
spit on him. When they threw seawater
on my back, I didn't scream.
Her memory alone is worth ten lashes.

Note: There is a grave in a small churchyard outside Plymouth, Tobago with the
inscription: 'Within these walls are deposited the bodies of Betty Stivens and her
child. She was the beloved wife of Alex Stivens who to the end of his days will
deplore her death, which happened on the 25th day of November 1783 in the 23rd
year of her life. What was remarkable of her was she was a mother without
knowing it, and a wife without letting her husband know it, except by her kind
indulgences to him.' No other known records of Betty Stivens exist.

OLGA

There were experiences between us
neither could imagine. It was when you said

you couldn't face potato skins because
of the memory of *Mama*

last seen huddled in a lorry
that it all spilt out. Camps,

living in fear, thankful for a skin,
clinging to a skirt, thankless for a life.

You looked worn so
I offered to bake potatoes.

The shudder made me hesitate,
I touched your arm.

You began to want to tell
and I began to want to know.

Opening a bottle of Jack Daniels,
it didn't matter that I was young, employed.

You paid three pounds an hour
though half your whisky was drunk.

We sat telling of lives,
lives lit with candles,

listening to *Wild Man Blues*,
pasta entwined round forks.

Tomorrow you'd go to Chambers
and I'd clean your rooms.

Wendy French

SWIMMING TOWARDS THE FLOW

He didn't know your history;
hadn't skimmed your notes.
Said he preferred to imagine you a fresh
young eel swimming against the tide.
He handed you a pair of ill-fitting trunks
and you proclaimed, *Like swim, Like swim*,
and stepping into the deep end of life
confidently disappeared to the bottom.

A sleepy afternoon, the alert life-guard
was with you in seconds and you rolled
and coughed on the slippery side
as youngsters sniggered. In Somalia
there are no signs warning of danger.
Written up clinically a vivid description
of the night the police pulled you in,
cold against the pull of the Thames,

struggling against water and uniforms.
Weeping, your father later translated
that the white angels of heaven floated upstream
and they enticed you to join them, flaunting
a message, that was held tantalisingly
just to the right of your life.

Wendy French

Snow melting our faces
we left all those Vermeers
behind locked doors, this time

we were too early. Hands frozen
together we hid disappointments
in woolly gloves.

You rationalised feelings
and said we'd seen
most of them anyway, before

and then you danced along cobbles
to make me laugh
pretending you were drunk

riding a bicycle into the Hofvijver.
And all I wanted was *The View of the Delft*;
the lady reading the letter.

Bryan Heiser

CANTO TWO: ON TOP OF THE WORLD

I'm writing this upon my word-processor
    Snug in my bungalow in Camden Town;
You know, Lord, what a bungalow is for?
    A dwelling with no upstairs, only down;
Ideal for those like us with no, or poor,
    Mobility? Come now, my Lord: don't frown –
A club foot isn't something you need hide:
One wears one's disability with pride.

A word-processor's quite another item:
    A marvel, though it now seems commonplace,
That stores my verses fast as I can write 'em
    (I've all my output in this little space),
Checks spellings, finds me rhymes – what's this: *ad litem*?
    I'm sorry, but that just won't fit the case –
Powered by electricity. Oh dear!
How many things there are to be made clear.

Let's just say electricity is power
    Sent where it's needed through a metal string
That lights like summer noon the midnight hour,
    That when I want makes Pavarotti sing,
Cooks food, pumps heated water through my shower,
    Raises my hoist and – not a little thing –
Keeps me alive when sleeping in my bed:
Without my ventilator I'd be dead

Since polio (Lord, there's another new one:
   An illness that I caught in Casablanca.
Astonishing, the harm that it can do one,
   And yet I look back on it without rancour.
It is perhaps a strange thought, but a true one:
   In some ways disability's an anchor:
It drags one back, but also keeps one grounded –
Though on the whole avoidance is well founded)

At twenty-seven (can it be a quarter-
   Century past?) left me quadriplegic:
Something in the air or in the water,
   And all I had with me was analgesic
(And much hashish – although we didn't oughter,
   We did: it made the scenery more . . . *scenic* . . .
Stocks had been running low, we had to score,
So flew from Venice to the Berber shore).

And then I went to Bruce's place in Philly
   And saw myself decapitate a chicken
(The neighbours made my squeamishness seem silly).
   Then some days later I began to sicken
Till nothing of me moved except my willy
   (Which never lost the chance to lift and thicken,
But I was twenty-seven – what the heck?),
My right hand and the bits above my neck.

This *was* a trifle scary, I admit it,
   But I maintained a British upper lip:
As long as circumstances would permit it
   I'd show how firmly I could keep my grip,
Though hardly anything would let me grip it,
   I'd so much tranquilliser in my drip
Unknown to me till – Jesus Christ! – the day
They took it, without telling me, away.

Then there were tears – though not without misgiving!
    But I digress. Here's what I want to say:
What therapists call 'Tasks of Daily Living',
    What people do unaided every day,
Technology – machines are made for giving –
    Lets me do in an automated way:
I move around, go to the toilet, sleep,
With squeak and whirr and intermittent beep.

I won a human race, but never ran it:
    Technology and luck kept me alive,
And living on the right part of this planet –
    Caucasians are likeliest to thrive,
And since the time that Greybeard first began it
    This is my hour: no way could I survive
If I had lived, my noble Lord, when you did,
Or came into the world when you, friend Hugh, did [. . .]

It's six a.m. I'm lying in my bed,
    A bed that operates by electricity
And at a button's push lifts feet or head,
    Where I've enjoyed – I'll be discreet – Felicity;
And by it on a table-top are spread
    Radio, 'bottles', drink and, of necessity
Because I fail to breathe when not awake
A box that takes the breath that I don't take.

From this machine an inch-wide plastic hose,
    Snaking across the gap, above the duvet,
Circles my head and hisses in my nose
    Sweet air more precious than the rarest *cuvée*,
Than which, I think, has never been *une chose*
    More painfully *perdue*, more gladly *trouvée*,
Except for life, and honour, and divinity,
Love, virtue and – no, one can't *find* virginity.

And, willy-nilly, here I stay till someone
   Arrives to get me up. The tasks include
A private wash (a genital and bum one),
   Getting me panted, trousered, socked and shoed,
And – this fazes the fainthearted or dumb one,
   But not the even moderately clued –
Sliding me on a plank of polished ply
Into my chair. And then we say goodbye.

Next to the bathroom (after cups of tea)
   Where defecating isn't problematic
Only because – I didn't get it free -
   I have a hoist: the type that's automatic
And tracks across the ceiling, lifting me
   Out of my wheelchair, mildly *katabatic*
('Produced by downward wind': admit, that's neat!)
And lowers me onto the toilet seat,

And off again. And then, from there, my day
   Is apparatus- and assistance-free
But for my chair (that mustn't go away)
   And charming taxi-drivers helping me
Into and out their cabs to work or play
   And colleagues making countless cups of tea –
Unless my programme suffers a *hiatus*
If later *katabasis* isn't *flatus* –

Till bedtime, when a helper comes again
   Slides me onto the bed and then undresses me
(Reliability can be a pain:
   The very thought of it sometimes depresses me;
But Joshua's a wonder, in the main)
   And sometimes it's my Lambkin who caresses me,
Puts me to bed and joins me for a tup:
There's going down before there's getting up!

Now, two last things before the moral's stated
   That brings this second Canto to its end;
A moral oftentimes reiterated
   Not least by Al, my quadriplegic friend;
A moral that's succinctly concentrated
   In radio transmitters that depend
(Or hang) around my bedside light and neck,
And save my ship from pirates, storm and wreck.

One, when I press it, opens my front door,
   The other calls emergency assistance.
Things that I thank God and the Council for –
   Without them I would not have gone this distance:
They would have found me lying on the floor.
   Thanks, Ivan, also for your stern insistence
I wear them when I'm indoors on my own,
Especially when in bed or 'on the throne'. [. . .]

And though I'll never walk again, or dance,
   Or score a try or jump or lift a bucket,
On Wednesday we go Eurostar to France
   And we'll have fun: the rest's not worth a ducat.
And if you think this not a proper stance,
   I'll tell you what my stance is: you can fuck it!
It isn't what you've got, it's how you use it:
If you define the race you needn't lose it!

Now, last, I see I've named one or two friends.
   I hadn't meant to, but I have, and so
I promise that before this letter ends
   I'll mention *you*; and if I don't – you know . . .
My memory . . . So let me make amends
   When next we meet. And meantime, let us go
Hand in whatever turns you on . . . and me,
Into a rather different Canto Three.

III

Chris Beckett

THE DOG WHO THINKS HE'S A FISH

It's on a plane that Harry tells me about his dog,
a Pointer with the long ears and square muzzle,
the strong, spare body that locks into position
like a well-oiled gun when it's primed to shoot,
except that Harry's dog not only likes to swim
like a labrador fetching ducks, but like a fish,
that is with his head immersed and eyes wide open
staring into the sea, coming up to Harry underwater
and shoving his nose up close, letting out a bark
that sounds like a small thud and sends ropes
of excited bubbles floating to the surface.
Never mind the legs thrashing and the tail trying
its best to wag and steer at the same time,
forget the lack of gills or of any attempt to sieve
a bodyweight of plankton through his teeth,
this is a dog who sees no difference between
himself and fish, enjoying the element of both
and a good shake between the two,
which isn't far removed from me and Harry
knocking back a drink and chattering
like sparrows as our plane takes off.

Chris Beckett

A hall in Addis Ababa, summer
1964, and Geraldine is dancing.

Back then, I was scared of her legs,
and this photo's got four of them,
shooting out of her blue tutu
like bolts of lightning from a clear sky.

It's as if she's only earthed
by her points, so fierce and graceful
is the charge running through both
of her twelve-year-old bodies.

Her career was over in an afternoon
like a summer storm, but Dad
was always proud of his shot:

best one I ever took, he'd say,
look, look, she's moving!

Meryl Pugh

THE LIGHTHOUSE KEEPER

They come in here every month without asking,
banging open the door with crates and voices.
I'll be up top with my pipe. I don't answer:
it's always the same. The noise as they dump their load
falters the further they wade into silence.
For a moment, you hear it invade them. Then off they go,
out past the beach where the boat is sulking,
onto the rocks, calling to gulls with purpose.
If I crane my neck, I can see the whole show;
the scratching of heads, the hands on hips. Only then
do I come down, treading the spiral
in my boots, heavy and slow so they'll hear.
It makes me laugh, the running inside,
the turning around on the spot as they watch me descend,
their faces like rock pools reflecting the sky.
I know why they really come. Supplies? Yeah, right.
I imagine them back on the mainland, peering from windows
to where that great arm punches through fog.
In their heads, in the tip of my magic wand, I am hoarding
Madeira, Marsala, Calvados, gold.

Meryl Pugh

WIG

They know I wear wigs.
They run down the road
after me, shouting
'Wig! Wig!'
I tried it back at them once:
'Small! Loud!'
They didn't like that.
Police didn't either:
'Bothering minors.'
At home, if I sit just so,
I can see, through the slot
in the curtain, the woman
next door in her garden.
She frowned at me once,
as I walked up the path
and she paced hers, like an orderly
down a ward. Her scissors were ready,
intent on catching that first eruption
out of her wealthy earth;
the bursting of tulips and daffs
from their pearls deep in the ground.
Inside, I sit with my skirt spread out,
in my favourite part of the room.
I peel off the wig like a chestnut husk
and the sun lights me up like an opal.

Meryl Pugh

THE SUNDIAL COLLECTOR

She arranges them around her room
not always where the sun will catch them.
Some tell her there is no time; only space,
emptying itself of stars and planetary bodies,
like a velvet curtain shaken free of dust.
Others are supposed to check the moon,
the zodiac's position in the sky
and from this, indicate the proper government
of nations. These ones need to be ornate,
well-carved, expensive and hard-won.
As light encounters the old glass
in her window-panes, it buckles,
falling in slow ruffles to slop all over
the sundial on her bed, persuading lovers
to stay longer. Some, tipped on their sides,
throw the time they catch down on the floor.
It folds like syrup poured into a flour well,
before leaking, drop after drop, between
the floorboards. The shop downstairs
often finds it has more time than it thought
and the shop-girls kick their heels as the clock
ticks and drags its hands towards five.
Her favourites are the polyhedrals:
a family of odd flowers, sprouting
from mahogany and oak, they tell her riddles
and bend their many faces to inspect her room.

Daljit Nagra

TRENDY WOMAN BLUES

'Why now not be naked? You naughty western woman!
Not four month since I aeroplane you over
and you're ordering newest Bombay passions
as a choice of ready-made clothes. What confusion!
Never in my village had we changed our sweater,
Jesus Creeper, made of gold kohl pot.
We were proud of it. But this tightening of the bottoms
of the costume of the dowry of the sacred day
is drain-piping when we should be baggy
with a widening pride of the cardboard
at the base of the pyjama – a meeting of two
puffed curves into a perfect Punjabi smile –
what you have puckered into a bony lady's bellybutton!

Turn off those sunglasses. Is it summer in the evening of winter?
Look at me – what is that cherry jelly
over the lash of your eyes? Are you bleeding upwards?
Those mascara scars? This half-cut hair mop?
Have I come home to a skinheading sex-change woman?

Even our peoples at the Sugar Puff factory,
I overhear the poison their wives at night monster
their crazy heads with: *She was in film star red* they say.
No, no, one says, *she's in chocolate sauce*, and another –
the blue boiler suit boy slaps his hands together,
choking, even louder starts: *No – no, no, no,*
I saw her at the broken biscuit stand
in the company of her Doctor, the Avon lady
and by all the Gods in my top pocket, he says,
I swear she was in English poodle pink!
And they laugh and they toss up their chappatis
at the lunchtime talk only of your toe nails.
I have to make up constipation for shame of leaving the loo!

You were the first English-reading, city wife in our long family
and you cheat me for a Green Card.
How could you so laughing last night
tie my once 'B' team hockey body
with the jockstraps unframed from the wall
(they were souvenirs from my College days)?
All night long – the beastly pouncing on my chest.
The tickling, the lipstick, the 'odour toilet'.
The neighbours of the terrace giggling. My father in a cough.
It was the worst waking from snores to screaming I ever make.
I can no longer meditate or pray or lock into my lotus position.
Even now, I can not close my legs!

O my *Rub*, what is England happening for us?'

Rub – God

95

Daljit Nagra

THE TRANSLATOR

'We were watching *Amar, Akbar, Anthony* on video
which is my dad's own dodgy copy. It's about three fit brothers
who are separated as kids and grow up in the religions of their
    names.
You must watch it Miss. You can get it with subtitles
and when Anthony, the Catholic one with his hair
flying blackly across our heavily mantled screen
was brown-eyeing Christ to ask for the address of his proper parents
and started to cross himself, I slid off our red leather sofa
and done a *Hail Mary, Hail Mary, Hail Mary,*
four-quartered myself then curtsied a little, you know,
to help Anthony with his miracle.

   Dad just stared at me,
knocking his turban side to side
that I almost thought it would come off
like it often does when he's doing his press ups and his face goes
    mauve
But he took off his flip-flop (the one with a broken thong),
held it in the air and started to shout in 'our' language: *What idiot!*
If you want to call on God, call on any one of our ten gurus.
Why ask white God's wife? Is she your mother?

Amar, Akbar, Anthony: Bollywood film of the 1970s

96

Sometimes he's got a really funny way – he says I've changed
and that he's going to put me in a Sikh school, a proper school.
That's why I did as my dad praised me to Miss.
While you were all doing Hail Mary at the end of assembly,
I first clasped my hands, knelt down,
prayed with this ditty my dad taught me,
imagined the Golden Temple
and our ten bearded Gods to your up-on-the-cross one then roared:
Wahay Guru!
Wahay Guru!
Wahay Guru!
Like that.'

Wahay Guru: blessed be God

Daljit Nagra

ON THE DEATH OF A FRIEND

(i.m. Sajid Naqvi)

'When my friend the muslim died of a freak heart attack
they took him to a mosque. We saw the naked body
in an ante-room being wiped and dressed into ethnic garments
(he used to wear black, gothic style clothes).
They oiled down his hair (he would have laughed at that)
and his varnished face in the open coffin around which we,
his university friends, after waiting for the nod, walked
and then sat dumbly looking on and listening to more Koran hymns,
thinking he would have preferred The Smiths.

Then we followed his hearse to a Shi'ite cemetery
amidst the tall tree'd roads of Surrey (he'd been living
with friends in Neasden and would have probably stayed there).
His relatives walked past us to guard over him
and his divorced mother who hadn't seen him for over a decade
had been flown from Delhi and his father from Derby
had taken charge of his only son, though he would have sooner
brought him back in line if he'd known
about the girlfriend he hid from a different caste.

Hearing the prayers like hard soil – overwhelming his coffin,
with all the surprises of the day, he no longer seemed
just one of us, he'd been packaged.
But like him, no matter what we become, I suppose
our backgrounds will come flying out of the woodwork
to see that we are given our own type of fitting ending.

It's just that it felt like a final insult,
the fake flush on his cheeks standing for his embarrassment
at being reduced to the one version of himself
with all his friends from all sorts of cultures
watching this Indiany-muslimy, obedient-boy side to him.
The lid come off the life he'd kept quietly away.'

Jo Roach

The day of cousin Eddie's funeral
weren't we all after being barred
from the 'I Go' and the 'Ramblers'.
Dick's eldest daughter Mary
passed us by up at the crossroads,
five brothers, tret no better than tinkers,
breaking the silence with did you hear
about Whelan, him that owned the old dog,
he'd a powerful temper on him,
lived up at Sally Noggin. A stroke.
Now then. And Micky Murphy, big strapping
lump of a man, great fisherman that he was,
him in his good suit too, just down from mass.
Heart attack. His wife's demented.
And young Donny O'Shea, no age at all,
light on his feet, go a round with anyone.
Imagine. Do you ever hear anything of Georgie?
Him that married the Sligo one.
And Jack here, home especially from England,
having nearly died himself
on the roughest crossing ever.
If poor Eddie were here now, God love him,
he'd be mortified at leaving us
with such a terrible thirst.

Jo Roach

ST PATRICK'S DAY POEM

When painting Roseanna's portrait
put weight on her
as though she'd often eaten
soda bread with buttermilk.
Stroke a blush on her cheeks
as if she were breathless from dancing
up at the Ballybrack crossroads.
Whiten her hands.
Straighten her back.
Leave out the lines on her face
and that pained look in her eyes,
dark as a priest's soutane,
by keeping the wedding-ring
out of the picture.
Put a shine on her black hair
as though I had brushed it.

Jo Roach

SAYING GOODBYE

On the doorstep, with
an armful of milk bottles
rinsed clean for the morning,
I see the doctor out: Dr Dalton
who wears a suit that doesn't fit,
the black frames of his glasses
hide his eyes, he's not a handsome man.
I ask 'When is she going to get better?'
He doesn't lie and I thank him,
still holding the bottles.

Jo Roach

THE SILVER TROPHY

His nicotined fingers tie fishing flies
of teal feather and rabbit fur,
his calloused palm dirty against
the glint of the metal hook.
He arcs the line across the lake
and waits. Rolls his own in one hand,
draws the paper over his tongue
with just enough spit to hold the edge.
Later, at the sound of him coming
in through the door, didn't Annie
and the young one, their eyes lowered,
lift the table and put it down
in front of him. Him with not one word
to say to those children of his, as he
clears his plate, then sets to;
guts the fish into a bucket,
swills his hands in the bloodied water.
I remember nothing of his dying, only
the darkness of Lough Ree and him fishing there.

Jo Roach

PLACE

As for words, he used so few
that his past was a high stone wall
leading down to the strand
and the smell of the sea
where fishermen never learned to swim.

He listened to a man from Wicklow play
runaway notes on his fiddle
in Camden Town or Kilburn
where the air was stale
in bars that were not home.

When my father's largeness left him
he went looking for a place to die
within walking distance of the sea
and the shadow of mountains
he could put a name to.

Dominic McLoughlin

THE FORD

We like this watery interruption to our journey.
We cycle with our feet up as high as handlebars,
praying momentum will carry us through.

Or we drive in the car, spraying the hedgerows,
wrecking the engine. *Please now test your brakes.*
Our fantasy of a dead end almost comes to be.

The road dives under water, holds its breath
for the time it takes for the stream to rush over it.
In summer, the sign's a reminder of days more plentiful.

We stand in the trough at the bottom of the hill.
We want to be swept away, or made to leap,
or made to turn back faced with deep waters.

Dominic McLoughlin

JUMPING FOR ST CHRISTOPHER'S

They tied an elastic band around my ankle.
Granted, it was two hundred feet long. I

took a deep breath and in a flash wished
I was performing a more elaborate stunt: say,

getting married at the same time. He checked
the knot, clapped me on the shoulder, said

You'll be alright! Now's the time to step off
into the void. I could have avoided this:

not returned the form, done lengths,
laps, played dominoes for hours on end. Still.

I put my best foot forward. Earth, I'm falling
towards you; coming close, not touching.

Dominic McLoughlin

FITTING

She made a jewellery box and a chest of drawers
for her friends from choice pieces of wood.
Knowing he wouldn't be seeing her for a while
he needed to make her something just as good

which could come to represent, given time,
days spent pushing friendship to the limit,
never hanging back on the killer line;
where form and function were a perfect fit

and which would force her to remember him.
So he made her a low coffee-table
that she would forever knock her shins on.
With stout legs in beech and a veneer in maple,

it was steadied by repeated dove-tail joints
which stood for how they'd flown, despite fixed points.

Dominic McLoughlin

HUMMINGBIRD

Tenacious brute in a small package.
Rufus male, a time bomb
on a short fuse. Never more

than half an hour from conking out.
Sucking up glucose through its curved beak –
life-giving sugar drip.

It has two settings: fast forward
and freeze frame, with a pause button on
while it sups from the artificial honey cup.

Equal and opposite wingbeats
each part of that high-octane dance
getting it where it wants to go: nowhere.

Whirr gives it stasis. Refuelling
by the hour, minute, second. Too fly to sing
it chirrups and growls, occasionally chatters,

frightening rivals wanting to muscle
in on its juice bar. Heavy hitter,
guzzling twice its body weight.

Then with a wink it's gone. Splashing out
on an ill thought out trip, a sojourn
down some good-for-nothing arroyo.

Really on the wing, winging it
like it never did, like a kid just running
for the sake of it.

Nadine Brummer

LARVA

I've not gone down on my knees
on a rock in the Himalaya
like the man I met tagging the bees
of South-East Asia.

I'd stopped, in the heat, to watch
how he put his ear to a crack
to listen for signals, to catch,
in his butterfly net,

feathered hairs tipped with pollen,
or bees, in pairs, spinning
in copulation or the swollen
ovipositors of a queen.

I thought a life could go by
without kneeling down to inspect
an insect's shins and thighs,
to know a different species

by its body-parts.
Then, this summer, I gazed
at a creature caught by the cat.
Not a worm or a snake

but a smooth, segmented body
reared up, on my hand, and I saw
how light came through its amber belly
and made it pearly as if

this crawling insect had a soul
not visible in egg or pupa,
nor even in the Death's Head imago
which enters any hive for honey.

Nadine Brummer

THE HILL

Opposite the house there's a hill,
a slope of two long fields up to a ridge
which I've watched for seventeen years
from the table. I've seen its neutral soil
passionately redden with poppies
or grass come lilac out of a mist.
I've heard bullocks cry on that hill
before seeing their bulk, the way
they nudge themselves along like boulders.
I've looked up to that hill,
looked up then looked away, to eat or talk
and I've turned my back on it
when the curtains were drawn.
Even a hill shut out exerts a pull –
you sense sky using it as a headrest.
In spring I've walked up a path
glinting with eyebrights and yellowhammers
for the view from a stand of beech.
Land falls away through the trees
into the valley and into that light place
you can't quite name on top of a hill.
This one has held my casual gaze
like the coin from a Roman soldier's pocket
which has just been uncovered.
It's only since leaving the house I realise
that the best view has always been
from indoors, from window-panes

squared like a grid to draw by.
I've seen the authority of fog
wiping out cattle, trees, grass, everything,
and then the hill come through again
like the idea of help.

Nadine Brummer

BLACKTHORN

I can't remember when we agreed
that the blackthorn this spring
had been better than ever,
or when it was that she said
'What does it mean?
It must mean something' –
as if every packed twig
were a sign,
like red skies at night,
or the berries she'd count on the holly.

I'm trying to recall
whether it was before or after she spoke
of her son dying
that we exclaimed about the hedgerows'
intensity of white,
and were not adequate
with words like 'snow' and 'drifts',
and 'dizzying',
and how 'the ground shifts'
when you walk amongst it.

Maureen Li

AUNTIE KATE'S WAKE IN MY PARENTS' HOUSE

Of course we went back to the house afterwards,
ham on the good plates, and every room
as cold and smaller than it was.
Look, I said, for something to say:
this is the room I slept in
when she came to stay

in her scratchy coat with the buttons
she polished on her sleeve and the hat that dipped
that she tried to make straight with the iron
and a cloth all steaming only it wouldn't
and she said what can't be cured
must be endured I always say. There was
a special colour came in when she came. They said
for her to have my bed and me the lumpy one
in the room with the funny smell
and the floor that made my slippers come off.
Sometimes she didn't come to stay
even when I counted and counted
the little hard buttons on the lumpy bed
like the noughts in noughts and crosses. One time
they went away on the train and she came
and she washed me in the sink
bubbles popping on my knees
and her slippy hands and her pink shiny frock
got wet all over and she didn't shout
she laughed and she said well
I wasn't born dry was I?

We shouldn't be standing here I said
with the mangle and the tea-cloths ironed in piles
and the cold.
We should be shaking people's hands and saying
yes she was she was.

Maureen Li

LOADING THE CARAVAN AGAIN

Opening our summers like champagne –
maps unfolded with a crack, the hiss
of tyres inhaling air, that headiness
that came on us as loading up began.

And oh such times we had! Remember when
the blank stare of the moon awoke us, and
silver shimmer where there had been sands –
a quilt of jellyfish laid over them.

The hand-rung warning of a tide that came
in like a fleeing horse. A dazed sea
lapping the van like milk. Pictures of me,
of you, shiny both of us with the same

lightly accepted grace, plain as day,
something we were entrusted with, and now
have lost, bewildered, not knowing how
to search for it, holding ourselves to blame.

Time for loading in an icy rain
your books on making kites, the motorbike.
The long division of it all is like
sorting my mother's button-box, and then

seeing the tidy colours run again.
Not that. Not the tyres on gravel, or
your screened face. Not the blurring lights. More
the caravan's dry imprint in the lane.

Bill Presley

Idwal Cottage, grey, rainy afternoon.
Down with the milk can to Emyr, Blaen Nant.
His sheep in mist come sudden through the gloom.
His talk's of subsidies, the usual rant,
his neuralgia. Toiling back up the track,
I see grey mist part, high on Y Garn,
then there's a lifting, disclosing black
rock pinnacles that dominate the farm.
I'm given my own lifting – of the heart
as the mists start flying, changing their tints.
Blown thin by blue wind, they clear a rampart,
teasing about the summit's imminence.

Lift! Let chapel bells time my heart again
in light tomorrow on Pen-yr-Olou-Wen.

Nell Keddie

PLENITUDE

This is the tree we planted near the pond last May,
a weeping willow-leaved pear chosen for its thick
anarchic growth and downy leaves, for which we dug
the ground, teased out the roots, lowered the rootball
into the hole and filled it back, the gardener
driving in an angled stake to tie the trunk
close to the surface of the soil to anchor the roots.
It's by moving the trunk grows strong, he says, treading
loose soil, raking mulch around the base.

I may not see this tree reach maturity.
I've lived here longer than anywhere
and I may die before it reaches half its height.
Now it has grown a foot, and the forsythia's gold
outside the kitchen door. This year I'll see flowers
come before the leaves. Already I'm thinking
of autumn when small brown fruits appear and the wind
lifts my neighbours' nets out from open windows.
I look up. The sky is blown with clouds.

Tricia Corob

ARCHES

As if we'd always been hungry
for arches like these.

To find them again
like friends we'd somehow

lost touch with.
The kind of friends

that make space for you –
you move through shadows

upward along the grain
of their ribbed pathways

soaring into aspirations
they've held for centuries.

The columns meet their opposites
high up, interleaving

long stone fingers
the way you once thought

destinies must be. But outside
gulls scream and newsprint

makes its own mosaic of the day.
Yet whatever was happening then –

the town under siege, starvation, plague –
here was a better world in stone.

Abundant fig trees and wheat
saints among curled lilies.

So we lean against these stones
as if we could be taken in by them

as the sun is, the body longs to be
folding into the folds of arches.

Diana Brodie

THE LAST TIME

The last time I saw you, I told you
he was dead. But this morning,
surrounded by wedding guests
in the sun-speckled churchyard, you,
looking spectacular in your white dress,
fizzing with lace and happiness,
asked me why he was not with me
and where he was today.

It seemed wrong to spoil the moment
and despite the tombstones that
surrounded us, inappropriate to say.
He's travelling, I said, which
perhaps is true. To lie well, one must
first convince oneself. But when I
came home, I was not prepared
to find him sitting in his favourite chair,
rocking gently, smoking,
reading Flaubert.

ACKNOWLEDGEMENTS

Matt Barnard: 'The Counterfeit Jew' in *Acumen*.
Chris Beckett: 'The Dog Who Thinks He's a Fish' and 'Double Exposure' in *Poetry London*.
Diana Brodie: 'The Last Time' in *Poetry Street*.
Nadine Brummer: 'The Hill' and 'Larva' in *HalfWay to Madrid* (Shoestring Press, 2002); 'Blackthorn' in *London Magazine*.
Robert Chandler: 'Elena' in *Poetry Review*.
Valerie Clarke: 'Jan Wandelaar – Drawing of a Skeleton' and 'G. B. Manfredini – Female Bust with Open Abdomen' in *Blue Nose Poets-of-the Year Competition Anthology 2001*.
Wendy French: 'Mauritshuis' in *Poetry File*; 'Olga' in *Smiths Knoll*; 'Swimming Towards the Flow' in *The Interpreter's House*.
Bryan Heiser: 'Letter to Hugh, Canto Two' in *Home* (ed. Kathleen McPhilemy, Katabasis, 2000).
Fawzia Kane: 'Tantie Diablesse Teaches Us How to Make Punch' in *Poetry Wales*.
Julia Lewis: 'Trees' and 'The Miracle' (under the title 'Remember That') in *PN Review*; Part I of 'Trees' in *Urthona*.
Maureen Li: 'Auntie Kate's Wake in my Parents' House' in *Smiths Knoll*.
Mary MacRae: 'Life Story' in *Magma*.
Daljit Nagra: 'Trendy Woman Blues' and 'On the Death of a Friend' in *Poetry Review*; 'The Translator' in *Stand*.
Meryl Pugh: 'The Lighthouse Keeper' in *Magma*; 'Wig' and 'The Sundial Collector' in *Poetry London*.
Jo Roach: 'The Watchmaker', 'St Patrick's Day Poem', 'Saying Goodbye', 'The Silver Trophy' and 'Place' in *Dancing at the Crossroads* (Hearing Eye, 2003).
Anna Robinson: 'Full Moon' (under the title 'Bubble Moon') in *the reater 4*.
Anne Ryland: 'Sea Script' in *First Eleven* (University of Newcastle Press, 2002); 'The Sister' in *The Interpreter's House*.
Deborah Sacks: 'Elise' in *Magma*.